This notebook
belongs to

_____

People with a best friend at work are seven times more likely
to fully engage in their work.

For maximum productivity, it's necessary that your desk is organized.

The average worker in America receives 200 email, paper,
and phone messages per day.

In a phenomenon called "karoshi," a high number of Japanese workers drop dead at their work desks due to their 60 to 70-hour workweeks. Every year, over 10,000 Japanese suffer "karoshi."

For every 1,470 resumes received, an employer will hire only one person.

The average workweek in the US is surprisingly only 34.5 hours.
But for the hardest working age range of 25-54, it is 40.3.

Charles Darwin invented the modern office chair. He added wheels to his own chair so that he could move around his office easier.

People who don't get involved in office politics are
more successful and efficient at work.

Reserved for Random Thoughts

Eighty percent of jobs are gained through networking.

More people walk or bike to work in Alaska than any other US state.

Nearly 80% of American workers are dissatisfied with their jobs.

Focused 90 minutes of work followed by a 20-minute break will make you much more productive. Also, look into "The Pomodoro Technique".

A professional typist's fingers travel 12.6 miles
during an average workday.

Laughter boosts your immune system by enhancing your antibodies and increasing your immune cell count. This helps reduce your chances of getting sick and missing out on work.

Listening to music while working actually helps people
get things done faster.

Staring at the green color can make you more creative and productive.

Always take notes during meetings because your brain
retains less than 5% of what is said. Need another notebook?

Holland has the shortest work week in the world
with only 29 hours per week.

By the age of 40, an average American has held
seven or eight different jobs.

Refrigerating rubber bands makes them last longer. Just let them adapt to the normal temperature change before stretching them too much.

Multitasking leads to increased stress, a 10% drop in IQ,
and as much as a 40% drop in productivity.

In 1968, Spencer Silver was working on creating a super strong glue. He failed and created a weak adhesive that left no residue behind. It took another three years to find a use for it – the Post-It note.

Reserved for Great Ideas

One quarter of office workers report a productivity
decrease in the summertime.

Almost 40% of young professionals in the US are so unhappy
with the lack of paid parental leave that they'd be willing
to move to another country because of it.

Monday is the most common sick day except in Australia.
Their most common sick day is Tuesday. G'day!

Nine out of ten Millennials are expected to change jobs
every three years. This means that most of them will have
15-20 jobs in their lifetimes.

It's a myth that NASA spent a million dollars to develop the space pen. The Fisher Pen Company did that on their own while creating it. Before 1967, NASA simply used pencils in space.

Employees who work under managers who integrate humor into their interactions report experiencing greater work satisfaction.

You can revive an old permanent marker by soaking it in a bit of rubbing alcohol until the ink starts to leak. Then, put the cap on and let it dry for 15 minutes. For regular markers, use water instead.

When office temperatures are low (68F/20C), employees make 44% more errors and are less productive than when it's warmer (77F/25C).

Employees who sit near a window are more productive
and are less likely to take extra days off.

Women business owners employ 35% more people
than all the Fortune 500 companies combined.

Leonardo Da Vinci is credited with writing the first resume.

The average office worker spends up to 50 minutes every day looking for lost files and other misplaced items. That's four hours a week, or about 200 hours a year – over eight whole 24-hour days!

Tuesday is the most productive day of the week.

Americans now spend more than 100 hours a year commuting to work.

Your brain can slow down dramatically with a mere 2% drop in your body water. Staying hydrated by drinking a sufficient amount of water or healthy liquids can increase your daily productivity by 14%.

Would you take a pay cut for a more light-hearted work environment?
55% of workers would take less pay to have more fun at work.

Reserved for the Bucket List

In 1965, executive pay in the US was 20 times higher than average worker pay. Today, executive pay is around 300 times the worker pay!

Multitasking at work can drop your IQ by 10 points!
That's the equivalent of losing one night's sleep or
twice the effect of smoking marijuana.

On average, US businesses spend $250,000 per year
to cover the costs associated with employee turnover.

You would need 507,000,000 Post-It notes to circle the world once.

Bosses who integrate humor as part of their management style create greater work performance, satisfaction, and cohesion amongst workers, and are perceived as better leaders and managers.

85% of all highlighters sold are yellow. It's in the middle of the visible spectrum of light and the easiest shade for the color-blind to see.

Adults who regularly get 7.5 to 9 hours of sleep
are up to 20% more productive.

Average workweek around the world is about 45 hours long.
Those in North Korea's labor camps work over 112 hours per week!

Breathing toner particles from photocopiers and printers is as bad for the lungs as smoking. It can also irritate your eyes, nose, and lungs.

A normal-size paper can be folded in half NO more than seven times. And thanks to exponential growth, if you WERE able to fold it 42 times, your paper would reach the Moon — literally!

Happy employees are 12% more productive than others.

More than 50% of lost work days are stress related, keeping approximately one million people home from work every day.

If you work 40 hours a week from age 21-65, you will work over 90,000 hours in your lifetime. That's about 14% of your life.

Forty percent of worker turnover is due to job stress.

Drinking alcohol in the amounts leading to a moderate intoxication level of .075 can boost creative thinking. Cheers!

Scissors were invented by the Egyptians in 1500 BC by fastening two bronze blades together with a metal strap. Romans picked it up around 100 AD and upgraded the design to the cross-blade style we use today.

If you eat unhealthy food, your productivity decreases as much as 60%.

The most popular day of the week to call in sick is Monday at 48% followed by Friday at 26%. Tuesday is the least popular with 11%.

Employees who have more control over the layout and design
of their workspace are healthier and happier at work.

Reserved for Doodling

www.ingramcontent.com/pod-product-compliance
Lightning Source LLC
Chambersburg PA
CBHW071324220526
45468CB00001B/484